when I was a
bridesmaid

Designer Fiona Walker
Commissioning Editor Annabel Morgan
Production Patricia Harrington
Picture and Location Manager Kate Brunt
Art Director Gabriella Le Grazie
Publishing Director Alison Starling

First published in the UK and the US in 2002.
Originally published in the United States as
When I Was a Flower Girl.

This edition published in 2011
by Ryland Peters & Small
20–21 Jockey's Fields
London WC1R 4BW
and
519 Broadway
5th Floor
New York, NY 10012

www.rylandpeters.com

Text, design and photographs copyright
© Ryland Peters & Small 2011

A CIP record for this book is available from the
British Library.

10 9 8 7 6 5 4 3 2 1

ISBN 978-1-84975-193-3

Jacket photography credits: cover photograph and spine
by Polly Wreford; back cover right by Paul Massey/flowers
by Jane Packer (www.jane-packer); back cover left and
centre by Craig Fordham.

Printed and bound in China

 For digital editions visit
rylandpeters.com/apps.php

when I was a
bridesmaid

Antonia Swinson

RYLAND
PETERS
& SMALL

LONDON NEW YORK

when I was a bridesmaid

This book belongs to ....

I live at ....

and am .... years old. I was a bridesmaid at the

wedding of .... and ...., which took place

at ....and afterwards at ....

.... on .... at ....

I know the bride and groom because ....

....

using this book

By filling in this book, you'll create a lovely record of your day that
you'll find fun to read in years to come. Write down as many details as
you can before the wedding and complete the rest soon afterwards —
it's surprising how quickly you can forget small details. Ask your mum
or dad if they will take photographs on the day of the things you want
to include. You might want to keep your wedding invitation, an order
of service and your place card from the reception, and you could also
try pressing or drying flowers from your bridemaid's posy.

place
photo
here

a photo of the bride and groom

Congratulations

being a bridesmaid

It's a great honour to be asked to be a bridesmaid. It shows how much the bride and groom like you and how well they think you'll carry out this important role.

   As a bridesmaid you're a member of the bridal party. Your main job is to help the bride and in this you may be joined by other bridesmaids your own age or older, and pageboys (you're known collectively as the 'attendants'). You'll travel to the wedding ceremony in a smart car (if you're very lucky it might even be a horse-drawn carriage!) with the other attendants and arrive before the bride. When the bride arrives, see if she needs any help with her dress or veil (though if she has any grown-up bridesmaids they'll do this), then get ready to follow her as she walks into the ceremony to meet the groom.

who's who at the wedding

The bride and groom
The stars of the day! Give them both a kiss after the ceremony and say a big thank-you for asking you to be their bridesmaid.

The best man
He is a relative or close friend of the groom and is there to help him. He looks after the wedding rings before the ceremony and stands with the groom during it. He also makes a speech at the reception.

The bride's father
He walks down the aisle with his daughter. (Sometimes the bride is given away by another male relative or a friend.)

The ushers
The bride and groom often ask some of their friends to help at the ceremony by handing out the order-of-service sheets and showing all the guests to their seats.

the other attendants

A bride often has several attendants at her wedding. Perhaps there'll be other bridesmaids of a similar age to you — your sisters or cousins, or daughters of friends of the bride and groom. There may also be pageboys, who'll also be about your age. The bride may have decided to have one or several grown-up bridesmaids — her sisters, perhaps, or her best friends. There's usually a chief bridesmaid or maid of honour (she's called a matron of honour if she's married).

The chief bridesmaid is the bride's main helper on the day. She makes sure that the bride's dress and veil aren't crumpled or creased before she walks down the aisle, and looks after the bride's bouquet during the wedding ceremony. The chief bridesmaid will also tell you where to go and what to do if you're not quite sure.

Preparations

my outfit

As a bridesmaid, you will wear a beautiful outfit chosen for you by the bride to go with her dress. Bridesmaids usually wear a special dress in a gorgeous fabric. The bride usually wears white or cream but bridesmaids often wear a different colour — a pretty yellow, perhaps, or pale pink or blue.

Whatever the bride chooses, she will probably ask you what you enjoy wearing so that she can be sure you'll like it. You might go on an outing to buy your clothes from a shop. If a dressmaker makes them, she'll need to measure you to make sure your dress fits perfectly. It's very exciting when you see your outfit for the first time and once it's ready you're bound to want to try it on. Just make sure you don't get it creased or dirty!

What my bridesmaid's outfit was like

✏

....

....

....

....

....

Where it was bought from or who it was made by

....

....

When I went to buy it or have it fitted

....

....

....

....

my hair and accessories

Pretty accessories will add the finishing touch to your outfit. If you are given new shoes for the wedding, it's important that they're comfortable, so say if they aren't. Practise wearing them at home so you can get used to them and ask your mum to rub the soles with sandpaper so you don't slip. Bridesmaids usually wear a headdress. This might be a circlet of flowers, a tiara, a decorated hairband or pretty slides or combs. Your hair will be arranged specially, either by a hairdresser or your mum. They'll also fix your headdress in your hair. Try not to fiddle with it — you want your hair to look perfect!

What my shoes were like

What my headdress was like

Who arranged my hair

the bride's dress

The bride wears a very special outfit for her wedding. The traditional choice is a long dress in white or cream, although some brides wear short dresses or even trousers, and some choose a different colour. Wedding dresses can be made in all sorts of wonderful fabrics, such as lace, satin, velvet, tulle or taffeta.

The bride usually keeps all the details of her outfit a big secret from everybody — especially the groom — until the morning of the wedding, so you'll have a lovely surprise when you arrive to get ready. Remember to tell her how beautiful she looks. If the bride's dress is very long and forms a train behind her, be extremely careful not to tread on it!

What the bride's dress was like

....

....

....

....

....

....

What her veil, headdress and shoes were like

....

....

....

....

....

place
photo
here

a photo of me in my dress

a drawing of me in my dress

the wedding rehearsal

Usually, there is a wedding rehearsal before the big day. Most brides and grooms feel a little bit nervous about the ceremony so the rehearsal is a good opportunity for everyone to find out exactly what happens when and what they have to do. The best man, the bride's parents and sometimes the groom's parents attend the rehearsal, along with the bride and groom. The attendants may also be asked to go along so that you're all familiar with the venue for the ceremony and can be shown where you'll walk and stand on the wedding day. If you don't go, don't worry — you'll be told exactly what to do on the day by the chief bridesmaid or another grown-up.

When the rehearsal was held ....

....

....

....

....

....

....

Who was there ....

....

....

....

....

....

The big day

getting ready

The wedding day has finally
arrived! You're bound to be
feeling very excited and perhaps
a little nervous, so take a few deep
breaths to calm yourself.

Eat a good breakfast so you
won't get hungry later and have a
nice bath. Perhaps your mum will
let you add some scented bubble
bath so that you smell delicious
and are squeaky clean!

You'll probably get ready with
the bride and all the other
attendants, and your mum or
a grown-up bridesmaid will help
you to get dressed. Resist the
temptation to put on your
wedding clothes too early — you
don't want them to get dirty or
crumpled. Once you arrive at the
wedding venue, smile and make
the most of every moment of this
special and happy day.

place
photo
here

a photo of me getting ready

the flowers

Beautiful flower arrangements are one of the things that make a wedding such a special occasion. The ceremony venue and reception are usually decorated with flowers — see how many you can spot and what they're like. Most brides carry flowers, which could be anything from a pretty posy to a big, spectacular bouquet. The groom, best man and ushers usually wear flowers in their buttonholes. You'll probably be given flowers to carry, perhaps in a little bunch or even in a basket or twined round a hoop. If you take them home after the wedding, you could try drying or pressing them as a keepsake.

What the flowers at the ceremony were like

What the flowers at the reception were like

What the bride's bouquet was like

What my flowers were like

the ceremony

At a religious ceremony in a church, the bride stands at the top of the aisle next to the groom, facing the minister. The minister takes the service, during which there are usually hymns and readings. At the marriage itself, the bride and groom make special promises ('vows') to love and support each other all their lives. Afterwards, the couple's parents, the best man and the attendants follow the bride and groom into a side room so they can sign the marriage register. When that's done, everyone processes back down the aisle and out of the church.

At a Jewish wedding in a synagogue, the bride and groom stand under a canopy or chuppah to be married by the rabbi. At a civil ceremony, a registrar takes the place of a minister. There may also be music and readings, though they won't be religious. You'll be expected to sit quietly during the wedding service, particularly the marriage vows themselves. Be patient - there will be time to chat and have fun later.

photographs of the ceremony

the reception

The reception is the party that follows the wedding ceremony. Sometimes the bride and groom greet the guests in a 'receiving line', standing with their parents at the entrance to say hello to everyone as they enter.

At the reception, food is served — perhaps a sit-down meal or a buffet, or canapés on trays. Speeches are given by the bride's father, the groom and the best man. It's traditional for the groom to thank the bridesmaids for doing such a good job!

The bride and groom will also cut their wedding cake. Once the first cut has been made, the cake is taken away and sliced up so everyone can try some.

Sometimes, there's dancing after the meal. The bride and groom's 'going away' is at the end of the reception.

Who I sat with

✏️
....

....

Who I talked to

....

....

What we ate

....

....

Who gave the speeches

....

....

What the cake was like

....

....

39

photographs of the reception

photographs of the reception

going away

All good things have to
come to an end, and
eventually it will be time
for the bride and groom to
leave for their honeymoon.
It's traditional for everyone
to gather together to say
goodbye and wave them on
their way. The bride and
groom sometimes change
out of their wedding
clothes into smart going-
away outfits and will
probably be driven off in a
car. They'll travel to their
honeymoon destination
the next day.

*a photo of the
bride and groom*

What time the bride and groom left 🖋 ....

....

What they wore ....

....

Where they went on honeymoon ....

....

place
photo
here

my favourite photo of the day

happy memories

You're bound to be very tired after such an exciting and fun day and to need a good night's sleep. The day after a wedding can seem a little flat and boring, but there are lots of things you can be getting on with.

This is a good time to write a thank-you letter to the bride and groom if they gave you a present. You can also fill in all the remaining bits in this book while everything's still fresh in your mind. Make sure that you write down all the things you liked best. In years to come you'll enjoy being able to re-live your special day as a bridesmaid.

What I liked best about being a bridesmaid

....

....

....

....

My favourite memory of the day

....

....

....

....

Photography credits

key: a = above, b = below, c = centre, r = right, l = left

Caroline Arber: 3, 12 al, 12 br, 15 ar, 15 br, 16, 17 r of c, 18–19, 29 r, 35, 44;

Craig Fordham: 2, 4, 6, 8, 9 r, 10, 11, 14, 15 al, 17 l of c, 17 cr, 17r, 21, 28, 30, 33, 36–37, 40–41;

Polly Wreford: 1, 7, 9 l, 9 cl, 9 cr, 9 r of c, 17 l, 17 cl, 23, 24, 26-27, 29 l, 29 l of c, 29 cl, 29 r of c,

38–39, 42–43, 46, 48; Viv Yeo: 9 l of c, 12 ar, 12 bl, 15 bl, 29 cr.

Publisher's Acknowledgments

Ryland Peters & Small would like to thank David and Annabel, Justin and Lizzie and Jamie and Berenice

for graciously allowing us to photograph their weddings. Many thanks also to Jane Durbridge.

Finally, a huge thank you to all our beautiful little bridesmaids.

Author's Acknowledgments

Thank you to David and Hannah for all their love and support, and to the helpful, efficient and creative

team at Ryland Peters & Small, in particular my editor, Annabel.